A Little Book About FEELINGS

From the award-winning
"RUBY'S STUDIO: THE FEELINGS SHOW"

ritten by:
bbie Schiller
mantha Kurtzman-Counter

ased on a screenplay by:
by Vanderzee,
mantha Kurtzman-Counter
Abbie Schiller

haracter design:
ine Mizushima

ook design:
en Pelletier

Copyright © 2011
The Mother Company
All rights reserved.
This book, or parts thereof,
may not be reproduced in
any form without permission.
www.themotherco.com
Printed in Malaysia
by Tien Wah Press January 2013
2nd edition – BkLitFeel20122
Library of Congress Control Number: 2012941266

THE MOTHER
COMPANY

Everyone in the whole
wide world has feelings.

Babies

Big people

Little people...

Even pets have feelings!

Feelings are reactions to things going on around and inside us.

Our brain sends messages
to our bodies, making us
feel different things.

You can see feelings on faces and bodies.

Or you can use words to express them.

If you share your feelings, other people can respond to them.

It feels so good when
people understand us!

Listen to what your feelings tell you.

Feelings are clues to help you understand what you need and who you are.

HAPPY

EXCITED

CURIOUS

PROUD

WORRIED

SAD

FRUSTRATED

SCARED

SURPRISED

We have so many different feelings and they change all day long.

When we share our feelings
and others understand us...

Our hearts feel full...

...of LOVE.

A Note to Parents and Teachers

Giving a child a basic understanding of feelings is among the most important jobs we have as parents and educators. Many of us have seen first-hand how tantrums subside and cooperation improves when children are able to effectively understand and express what they feel. Research shows that helping children develop emotional literacy before age five sets them up for more success in school, relationships, and life in general.

In this book, we encourage children to recognize the wide range of human emotions in order to help establish empathy and compassion ("everyone in the whole wide world has feelings"). Children find it comforting to learn that feelings are transitory and will not stay with them forever ("we have so many different feelings and they change all day long"). In addition, they benefit by knowing that universally some feelings are "achy and uncomfortable" and some are "light and warm," but all are ok.

Our children can be better understood – and in turn, feel more loved – by learning how to appropriately recognize, express and move through their feelings. After all, "when we share our feelings and others understand us, our hearts feel full of love." Isn't that true for us all?

— *Abbie Schiller & Sam Kurtzman-Counter, The Mother Company Mamas*

Guided by the mission to "Help Parents Raise Good People," The Mother Company offers world-renowned expert advice for parents at TheMotherCo.com, as well as the "Ruby's Studio" line of award-winning products for children.

THE MOTHER
COMPANY

Hi, I'm Ruby!
What's your name?

The Mother Company Presents
RUBY'S STUDIO
Social & Emotional Learning For Kids

Ruby's Studio is a line of helpful, fun, award-winning products designed to enhance communication, cooperation and self-understanding in young children.

ile Apps/eBooks

Videos

Handmade Dolls

Music

My Feelings
Activity Book

Sally Simon Simmons'
Super Frustrating Day

Find this and more at RubysStudio.com!

"A must in every
young child's library"
– Betsy Brown Braun

"We love Ruby's Studio"
– Jennifer Garner

"Edutainment at its best"
– Daily Candy